Original title:
Life's Like a Sandwich, It's What's Inside That Counts

Copyright © 2025 Creative Arts Management OÜ
All rights reserved.

Author: Isaac Ravenscroft
ISBN HARDBACK: 978-1-80566-047-7
ISBN PAPERBACK: 978-1-80566-342-3

Savoring the Moments

In a world of crust and filling,
We nibble on the silly things.
Pickles dance, and mustard's thrilling,
Joy grows rich in tasty flings.

Lettuce laughter, tomatoes cheer,
Each bite a chance to simply play.
The gooey bits bring us near,
Making sandwiches our kind of way.

The Centerpiece of Being

The bread may be just plain and white,
Yet, inside, a party brews.
With every layer, what a sight!
Who knew veggies could amuse?

Cheese grins wide, and bacon giggles,
A crunchy crunch, a secret tease.
Together they join in friendly wiggles,
Creating bites that aim to please.

Whispers Between the Breads

Between the slices, stories dwell,
Conversations seasoned just right.
Jokes and tales, oh what a spell,
As flavors flirt in playful light.

Surprises hide in every spread,
A swirl of mustard, a dab of jam.
Each munch brings laughter, visions fed,
In this unorthodox little slam.

Unwrapping What Matters

With each wrapper that we pry,
Laughter tumbles, like fresh bread,
In the crunch hides a giggling sigh,
What's inside? A feast well-spread!

Bites of joy in every slice,
Mayo dreams and crunchy swirls.
Unwrap the moments, don't think twice,
In this sandwich life, the fun unfurls.

Filling the Void

Grab a bun, don't be shy,
Slap on some mayo, oh my,
Lettuce winks from a crunchy heap,
It's a tasty secret we keep.

Pickles dance, ketchup swirls,
Catch that mustard like a whirl,
Layer it thick, don't go light,
With a bite, everything feels right.

Beneath the Crust

Under the layers, stories unfold,
Beneath that crust, magic is bold,
A dash of whimsy, a sprinkle of glee,
Sandwich tales shared over tea.

Rude tomatoes frown with a pout,
While cheese smiles bright without a doubt,
Greens giggle as they peek and pry,
Between each slice, joy is nestled nigh.

Taste the Essence

Savor each bite, what a delight,
Crunchy, munchy – feels just right,
Ignore the crumbs that mask the fun,
This silly feast has just begun!

With every layer, flavors entwine,
A jigsaw puzzle, gourmet design,
So raise your fork, let's dig in,
Beneath these layers, we all win!

Ingredients of the Soul

What's the secret to that zest?
A pinch of humor, that's the best!
Thick or thin, we spread it wide,
Joy and laughter, what a ride!

Dashing dreams, a sprinkle of cheer,
Craving happiness, we all steer,
Wrap it up, hold it tight,
In this feast, everything's right.

The Crunch of Experience

In the kitchen of our days,
We pile on all our quirks,
With laughter as the bread,
And memories as the perks.

Sprinkling joy like spices,
Oh, what a zesty treat!
Each crunch a little surprise,
Makes life's banquet complete.

Beneath the Layers of Time

Peeling back the onion skin,
With tears that make us laugh,
Finding flavors sweet or tin,
In the grand ol' photograph.

Old mustard meets new relish,
In the fridge of bygone days,
Each layer tells a story,
In its own peculiar ways.

Nurturing the Inner Feast

Tickling taste buds gently,
As we whip up our delight,
With every bite we take,
We savor silly sights!

From pickles to a cupcake,
Our plates brim with great fun,
The secret's in the laughter,
And the joy we've just begun!

A Journey of Flavorful Encounters

Oh, the roads we meander,
With condiments galore,
Each stop a brand new flavor,
And the smiles we can score.

Adventures in the pantry,
Can lead to wild surprise,
From peanut butter bashes,
To jellybean-filled pies.

The Palette of Existence

In a world full of layers, oh so bright,
Each flavor whispers, 'What's in me tonight?'
Pickles of humor, tomatoes so bold,
Creamy dreams hidden, treasures untold.

Jelly of giggles, mustard of cheer,
A sprinkle of joy, we hold so dear.
Crunch of the lettuce, so fresh and so green,
Every bite savored, what a quirky scene!

Filling the Gaps

Bread may be basic, yet it holds so much,
Jams of ambition, a tangy touch.
Slicing through worries, a savory spree,
Stacked with affection, just wait and see!

Crisp fries beside it, a side of delight,
Each moment we bake, we're rising to height.
Filling the gaps with laughter and cheer,
Dishing out memories, sincere and clear.

Dressings of Delight

A drizzle of laughter, a dollop of fun,
Ketchup of kindness, we spread 'til we're done.
Wrap it in friendship, let flavors collide,
Dip in the joy that we've chosen to ride.

Mayonnaise moments, smooth and so neat,
Tasty adventures, in unity sweet.
Hold on to the goodies that ooze from within,
Each bite we take shows how much we've been.

The Crust and the Cream

From crusty beginnings to creamy delight,
Each texture reveals our whimsical flight.
Underneath layers, a rich filling's found,
Savoring stories that dance all around.

A sprinkle of humor, a touch of the surreal,
Nature's own recipe, what's truly ideal.
Crunchy and smooth, we mix and we play,
Eating up moments, brightening the day.

Beyond the Outer Layer

Bread is just the case,
But here's the funny chase,
What's hidden deep inside,
Where the true flavors abide.

Lettuce adds a crunchy flair,
Pickles make you stop and stare,
Tomato gives a juicy burst,
Inside, it's where we quench our thirst.

Simple Pleasures

A plain slice can bring such cheer,
With toppings, it's a grand premiere,
A bite of this, a taste of that,
Oh, how I adore my spat!

Mustard dances, mayo glides,
In this feast that joy provides,
Simplicity can bring delight,
As flavors mingle day and night.

Rich Flavors

Beneath the crust, a treasure trove,
A mix of tastes in which we've rove,
Cheese that melts, and meats so bold,
In layers, stories do unfold.

A bite of sweet, a touch of spice,
In every crunch, oh so nice,
Richness can't be just the hue,
It's the mix that makes us chew!

The Stuff That Sticks

Peanut butter, jam so sweet,
Stickiness that can't be beat,
The odds and ends all blend in cheer,
Together they make memories dear.

Leftovers piled high anew,
Strange concoctions, if you knew,
Yet in this mess, we find delight,
In every nibble, a funny bite.

Spice of Existence

Seasoned well with laughter's zest,
In the middle, we are blessed,
A pinch of joy, a dash of fun,
Together, life is never done.

Chilli flakes on dreams so grand,
Garlic whispers, tasty planned,
With every bite, we dance and sing,
In our hearts, flavors take wing.

Craving Connection

In a world of layers stacked so high,
We often forget to stop and try.
Between the bread, what's truly sweet,
Is the laughter shared and friends we meet.

A pickle here, a spread or two,
Sometimes it's chaos, sometimes it's stew.
Yet every bite brings us so near,
To savor joy, let's raise a cheer!

Exploring the Inner Bowl

Digging deep in a bowl that's wide,
There's more to find beneath the tide.
Nuts and seeds, they come alive,
In every crunch, we learn to thrive.

A spoonful of fun, a dollop of glee,
Mix it all up, come dine with me!
The core's where the flavor starts to play,
Let's feast on laughter, come what may!

A Symphony of Ingredients

Each ingredient whispers with delight,
As they gather round in the kitchen light.
Tomatoes sing, and onions dance,
Together they create a savory romance.

If mustard's sour, it learns to blend,
Ketchup's sweetness, a zest we send.
In this medley, a harmony grows,
A funny tale that everybody knows!

Inner Warmth

In the heart of a sandwich, warmth is found,
A cozy feeling that knows no bound.
With layers of laughter and bits of cheer,
Every bite whispers, 'We're glad you're here!'

Cheese melting softly, embraced by the bread,
Jokes that are told and memories spread.
When it's all mixed, oh what a sight,
We find our warmth and hold it tight!

Dishing Out Depth

In a world full of layers, we often forget,
It's the quirky fillings that make us reset.
Pickles of laughter, mustard of cheer,
Spread on some joy, it'll keep us near.

Toppings of trials, a sprinkle of fun,
Every bite savored, we're never outrun.
From sweet to savory, life's tasty blend,
Each moment we munch, let the smiles extend.

The Texture of Existence

Crunchy or soft, we all have a style,
Sandwich of stories, each with a smile.
The bread may be plain, but the heart is bold,
With flavors of mischief, our tales unfold.

A dash of the silly, a spread of the wise,
With quirks in our layers, we're quite a surprise.
So stack it up high, don't worry or pout,
In the feast of our tales, we laugh it all out.

Squeeze of Essence

The best bits of life come with a squeeze,
Mayo of moments, like a warm summer breeze.
The essence inside is where joy resides,
Scoop out affection, let laughter be our guide.

Some say we're messy, but that's just their view,
With crumbs on our shirts, we're still shining through.
For each squeeze we share, is a treasure, it's true,
In the sandwich of being, it's all about you.

Feast of the Heart

Gather around for a hearty delight,
Chow down on dreams, with flavors so bright.
Between every slice, there's magic to find,
A banquet of blessings, with laughter combined.

The cheese of compassion, a hint of surprise,
With every good moment, our spirits will rise.
So let's raise a toast, to the moments we chart,
In this grand celebration, the feast of the heart.

Flavors of the Soul

Pickles in the pantry, a surprise delight,
Sweet jams and spicy mustard, oh what a sight!
Layered with giggles and sprinkled with cheer,
Taste buds dancing, there's nothing to fear.

Bread that's a little crusty, but still a treat,
Lettuce crisp and funny, not skipping a beat.
Add a dollop of laughter, and sprinkle of fun,
Savor the moments, life's just begun.

What Lies Beneath the Surface

On the outside, we might seem a bit plain,
But inside we're bursting like ketchup on grain.
A dash of adventure, maybe a quirk,
Hiding beneath, where all the laughs lurk.

From soggy old bread to gourmet delight,
Each bite tells a story, a flavor so bright.
Peanut butter dreams mixed with jelly's embrace,
Unwrap the layers, find joy in the space.

The Secret Sauce of Being

A drizzle of chaos, a sprinkle of zest,
Stir in the laughter, it's truly the best.
Whisked with emotions and seasoned with care,
The secret sauce of life is the joy that we share.

Mayonnaise moments and tangy surprise,
Blend together laughter beneath cloudy skies.
Bite into the magic, let it take hold,
A recipe for living, more precious than gold.

Unseen Ingredients of Joy

What lies in the layers, the crisps and the crunch,
Unnoticeable wonders that pack quite a punch.
Chocolate chips hidden in a savory roll,
Beneath every surface, there's a vibrant soul.

With each gleeful mouthful, we're smiling inside,
Sharing our stories, our hearts open wide.
So savor the moments, the laughter's delight,
For joy's in the fillings, it makes life just right.

Gusto and Gratitude

With layers of joy, we pile it high,
Mustard and laughter, pizza and pie.
A dollop of kindness, a sprinkle of cheer,
Munch on the moments that bring us near.

Cheese that melts with a hearty grin,
Bite into blessings, let tasty wins begin.
Tomatoes of gratitude, so juicy and red,
Savor each flavor, let joy be widespread.

Inviting Emptiness

The picnic's laid, but wait, oh dear,
A plate of just air? Let's shift the gear.
Grab a thin crust and decorate it right,
Imagination toppings, let's fuel the night.

A wish on a cracker, a dream in a bowl,
In this feast of nonsense, we swallow our soul.
Peanut butter worries, jelly of cheer,
Who needs a sandwich when friends gather near?

Crafting Connections

With bread of banter, let's make a toast,
Sharing our stories, what matters the most.
Layer by layer, we build and we bond,
In this feast of friendship, we all respond.

A pinch of humor, a slice of the fun,
Wrap up the laughter; the meal's just begun.
A dash of support, we spice up the talk,
In every delicious chat, we happily walk.

The Comfort of Companions

Together we munch, with giggles and glee,
A buffet of memories, just you and me.
Sourdough sorrows and rye bread delight,
Truly, each moment feels wonderfully right.

Mayonnaise moments, sweet pickles in line,
Each bite feels cozy, a taste so divine.
With crunchy compassion and warm, hearty cheer,
We feast on connections that keep us near.

Wholesome Inward Reflections

Beneath the crust, a treasure hides,
Pickles and giggles, where joy abides.
Lettuce of laughter, spread thick with cheer,
In the heart of the meal, all flavors draw near.

Mustard and mayo compete in the game,
Each squeeze a whimsy, none ever the same.
With each tasty bite, absurdities flow,
In the center of sandwiches, life's quirks steal the show.

Culinary Insights of Being

Mayonnaise dreams slathered on bread,
While surprises and snacks dance in your head.
Tomatoes spill secrets, crisp and so bright,
In the layers of madness, there's always delight.

A sprinkle of humor, a dash of the absurd,
Yummy reflections await to be stirred.
Inside this creation, flavors unite,
Crafting a moment of pure appetite.

Toasting to Inner Richness

Raise your glass to the gooey delight,
To fillings that twinkle and flavors so bright.
With every big bite, we chuckle and grin,
For the heart of the matter is where we begin.

Cheeses and veggies all dance on the plate,
Tasting the joys that we all celebrate.
Wrap it in laughter, let toppings abound,
In the heart of the feast, true riches are found.

Edible Epiphanies

In the layers of bread, wisdom is spread,
Ketchup of knowledge oozes from our head.
Crunchy realities, chewy and spry,
With burgers of banter, we all laugh and sigh.

Beneath every topping, a story awaits,
Munching on moments, tasting our fates.
From condiments crazy to buns soft and sweet,
The inner delights make our journey complete.

Tastes of the Heart

In a world of flavors, we all take a bite,
Some prefer peanut, others delight in the bite.
But the jelly that sticks, oh it spreads much joy,
Laughter and mustard, our favorite ploy.

Cheese melts with stories, each slice a surprise,
Pickles and jokes, they dance 'neath the skies.
Together we munch on this banquet of glee,
It's the giggles and toppings that set our hearts free.

Whispers in the Midst

In the middle of chaos, a crusty old roll,
Whispers of friendship, that nourish the soul.
Tomato as laughter, it drips with delight,
While onions may weep, we're still shining bright.

So grab us a platter, let's make quite a feast,
With quirky combinations, to say the least.
A dash of silliness, a sprinkle of fun,
In the heart of our gatherings, we become one.

Slices of Meaning

A slice of fresh avocado, so creamy, divine,
Next to witty banter, everything's fine.
Bread crumbles beneath us, but never the cheer,
We spread joy like butter, for all to adhere.

With each crunchy layer, let memories build,
Like a sandwich stacked high, we're always thrilled.
In flavors and laughter, we make our own way,
Adding zest to our journey, come what may.

The Core of Connection

Beneath all the layers, we find what we seek,
Shared moments as treasures, so sweet, not so meek.
Lettuce and laughter, they lift us each day,
In this feast of togetherness, we find our way.

So toast to our friendships, with crusty old bread,
Each bite is a memory, both tasty and spread.
Together we'll savor each quirky delight,
For in the great mix, our hearts take flight.

Hearts of the Harvest

In the garden, laughter blooms,
With veggies dressed in funny costumes.
Radishes wear hats, carrots dance,
While peas in pods share their odd romance.

Tomatoes giggle in sunlit rays,
Whispers of joy in leafy ways.
Each harvest tale, a savory song,
Reminding us where we all belong.

The Unseen Spice

In the kitchen, chaos reigns,
Whiskers on cats, and flour stains.
But in the pot, there's something neat,
A sprinkle of laughter makes it a treat.

Salt and pepper play peek-a-boo,
Dancing together, both old and new.
It's the giggles simmering in the heat,
That makes the dish feel so complete.

The Comfort Within

Nestled warm in a cozy bun,
Beneath the toppings, oh what fun!
Pickles parade and onions prance,
Each bite's a silly, scrumptious dance.

Spoons may wobble, bowls might spill,
But laughter's the spice that we all fill.
In every crunch and fluffy bite,
Comfort greets us, pure delight.

What Makes Us Whole

Chocolate chips in doughy hugs,
Peanut butter gives sticky shrugs.
Together they bloom, a sweet surprise,
Just like friendships, they harmonize.

Syrup drizzles on pancake stacks,
Waffles giggle with syrupy sacks.
It's the toppings stacked in tasty roles,
That remind us what truly makes us whole.

Delving into Delight

Grab a slice of fun, don't let it slip,
Add a dollop of joy, give it a whip.
Lettuce laugh all day, tomato cheer,
Pickles of delight, no room for fear.

Spread some humor thick, like creamy spread,
No bland bite here, just smiles instead.
Crispy thoughts crunch, in every bite,
Tasty moments linger, a true delight.

Tastes of Togetherness

Gather 'round the table, let's create a feast,
With silly jokes and laughter, we'll never cease.
A pinch of chatter, a sprinkle of glee,
Together we savor, for all to see.

Bite into memories, so fresh and bright,
The flavor of friendship, a pure delight.
Each layer we add, rich and profound,
In this banquet of life, joy can be found.

A Recipe for Meaning

Take the crust of dreams, brown and toasty,
Fill it with laughter, never too ghostly.
Slather on kindness, a generous spread,
Serve it with warmth, and happiness bred.

Chop up some antics, mix in some cheer,
Fold in the quirks, keep the absurd near.
In this funny dish, whatever you do,
Don't skimp on the fun, let it stew!

The Heart's Hidden Seasoning

Inside this feast, there's a secret flair,
A pinch of silliness, floating in air.
Marinate moments, let laughter thrum,
Season each bite, let the giggles come.

With every layer, the texture is right,
A flavorful collage, glowing and bright.
Taste the connections, oh so divine,
For the heart's true seasoning, is love intertwined.

The Secret Spread

In the pantry, secrets lie,
A jar of pickles that can't tell why.
Mayonnaise with a hint of sass,
A sandwich needs more than just the grass.

Tomato slices, juicy and bright,
With laughter adding flavor, it feels just right.
Throw in some mustard, a dash of cheer,
The spread of joy is what brings us near.

Flavor of Existence

Life's a buffet, stacked up high,
With layers of dreams that never run dry.
A taste of laughter, a sprinkle of zest,
In this quirky kitchen, we're always blessed.

Old bread crumbles, but still it's good,
A bite of adventure, it's understood.
Slather on kindness, don't keep it plain,
For every sandwich, there's joy in the grain.

The Core of Being

Beneath the crust, there's a heart so bold,
With stories unfolding, yet to be told.
Lettuce whispers secrets, crunchy and green,
In every good meal, there's magic unseen.

Cheese melts dreams on a warm toasted note,
While olives sit quietly, learning to float.
Pick a good partner, here's a wise tip,
A sandwich is better when shared with a trip.

Tasting the Truth

What's the real flavor when all's said and done?
It's laughter and friendship, that's how it's won.
So spread out your joys, let them blend and swirl,
In the sandwich of life, give it a twirl!

Chips on the side and a soda to sip,
Adding crunch to the fun in this little trip.
So grab a big bite, enjoy every piece,
In the midst of the chaos, let's find our peace.

Palette of the Heart

A slice of joy, a dash of glee,
Mix in some laughter, perfectly free.
Spread the kindness, layer it thick,
Toss in a joke, it's our favorite trick.

Colors unite in a whimsical way,
Brightening up the dullest day.
The quirks and the quirks, they play in the mix,
Painting our story with funny little tricks.

Scoop up the moments, piled high with cheer,
Craving the oddball, always near.
For every odd taste, there's sweetness to find,
In the palette that dances, so fun and unlined.

So grab a plate, and come take a bite,
Garnished with giggles, it's pure delight.
With each flavor that joins in the fray,
We savor the silly, come what may.

The Best Ingredients

A pinch of courage, a sprinkle of flair,
Whisk it together, beyond compare.
Add a dollop of silly, mix in with zest,
The secret concoction, feel truly blessed.

Bread of warmth, crusty yet soft,
Whipped cream of dreams, oh, how we scoff!
Chopped up the worries, sautéed with care,
The best ingredients, we gladly share.

From tangy to sweet, in layers they stack,
Creating our feast, no fun we lack.
So while the world simmers, let's toss in a pun,
For laughter's the glue, that holds us as one.

Resilient the filling, despite how it bends,
Embracing the chaos, where joy never ends.
Gather round the table, let the wild things inspire,
In this quirky buffet, we never tire.

Embracing the Crunch

Crispy giggles and giggles so loud,
Crunchy mischief draws in the crowd.
Let's munch on the laughter, savor the cheer,
With every delightful chomp we hold dear.

Layered with fun, a crunch of surprise,
Nibble on dreams, watch worries capsize.
Pickles of wisdom, stacked high on toast,
The more that we savor, the more we can boast.

In the midst of a crunch, we find light and grace,
Each bite an adventure, a joyful embrace.
So bring on the raucous, and raise up a toast,
For life's in the layers, that we love the most.

Tumbling and rumbling, the flavors collide,
With humor at hand, there's no need to hide.
Let's crunch through the chaos, in laughter we trust,
To enjoy every moment, is an absolute must.

The Sweetness of Substance

Creamy kindness, a dollop of flair,
Spread it around, in the flavor we share.
Juicy surprises, sweet as a dream,
Savoring life's moments, a delightful scheme.

Biting into joy, sugar-coated fun,
With every soft layer, our hearts weigh a ton.
Toffee-coated memories, melting with ease,
Sharing the sweet, like a gentle breeze.

Syrupy laughter drizzled on top,
Crumbs of companionship, we never drop.
Gathering around to taste every slice,
Life's best treasures are oh so nice.

So raise up your forks, let's dig in with glee,
In this feast of wonder, just you and me.
With layers of sweetness and hearty delight,
Let's revel in flavors that feel so right.

Essence of the Everyday

In a world where crusts can crunch,
We gather filling for our lunch.
Pickles of laughter, mustard of cheer,
The mix of the mundane, oh so dear.

A sprinkle of joy atop a base,
In sandwiches grand, we find our place.
Bread sometimes stale, but fillings new,
With every bite, we start anew.

Tomatoes of wisdom, lettuce of fun,
In each little nibble, we've just begun.
Between the layers, stories unfold,
In bites of the silly, our hearts turn bold.

A dash of mishaps, a slather of dreams,
The textures in life are more than they seem.
So gather 'round for a whimsical feast,
For the stuff that we cherish is what makes us least.

Unveiling the Heart's Fables

Beneath all the toppings, there lies a tale,
Of hiccups and giggles, our friendships scale.
Onions that bring tears and laughter alike,
In stories we munch, life's quirks take a hike.

Each bite is a chapter, thick, thin, or wide,
We feast on the memories, side by side.
The world's full of fillings, spicy or bland,
What's wrapped in this bread? It's all grand!

Sometimes we find a few crumbs of despair,
Yet all in the mix, there's joy we can share.
A taste of adventure, a hint of regret,
Like sharing a joke that we won't forget.

So unwrap your sandwich of moments today,
Embrace all the flavors that come out to play.
For in this great blend of the odd and divine,
We savor the essence, the heart in the rhyme.

The Goodness Within

Inside this creation, of bread and more,
Lies a rainbow of flavors, a savory chore.
Lettuce of kindness, tomatoes of grace,
In each juicy layer, our smiles we trace.

Surprises abound in this culinary dance,
With dressing of humor, we take our chance.
Peanut butter giggles, jellylike glee,
The delights that we hide, in fun we agree.

Pickle of patience, a dash of good cheer,
We pile on the goodness, hold it quite near.
With mustard of mischief, we spice up our fate,
For joy is the filling we do celebrate.

So come take a bite of what truly matters,
In each hearty sandwich, it's laughter that flatters.
With layers of chaos, and whispers of love,
The goodness within us, fits like a glove.

What Lurks Beneath the Surface

Beneath the crust, what secrets be?
A slice of confusion, perhaps, you see?
Yet hidden within a droll little tale,
Like a pickle that's sour but makes you exhale.

A bite of the unexpected, a crunch here and there,
Unveiling the layers of how much we care.
With soggy bottom stories and crispy delights,
Our hearts share a wink in the middle of bites.

Between bites of challenge and slather of fun,
The essence of who we are weighs a ton.
In the mix of the silly, the heartfelt, the sweet,
We explore what's beneath, with every treat.

So dig in with laughter, and unwrap the thrill,
For what lurks beneath is a banquet to fill.
As flavors collide in this humorous rush,
We find the joy hidden in each crunchy hush.

Inner Richness

The bread may look plain, it's true,
But wait until you find what's new.
Within the crust, delights reside,
Flavors and dreams that can't be denied.

Pickles of laughter, a spread of cheer,
Tomatoes of joy, so bright and clear.
Lettuce of hope, so crisp and green,
Layered with memories, a tasty scene.

So when you munch, don't judge the crust,
For hidden treasures are a must.
Take a big bite, savor the thrill,
It's what's within that gives you a chill.

Slices of Time

Each slice a moment, a jam-packed spree,
Peanut butter days, wild and free.
Some may be sticky, some just a breeze,
With crumbs of laughter, we do as we please.

Tomato slice stories, juicy and bright,
A sprinkle of chaos, oh what a sight!
Chomping on memories, sweet and sour,
A sandwich of seconds, devoured by hour.

So hold on tight as flavors collide,
In this layered journey, let joy be your guide.
Every bite counts, through thick and thin,
As we dive through the fillings, with a cheeky grin.

What's Buried Beneath

Oh, the crust is tough, but fear not my friend,
Beneath lies a treasure that twists and bends.
Mysterious fillings, surprises galore,
Dive in with gusto, explore and implore.

Jelly of memories, sweet as can be,
Mustard of mishaps, oh so zesty.
A pickle of wisdom, tangy and bright,
With each little bite, we're in for a delight.

So peel back the layers, and lift up the lid,
For tasty adventures await, yes they did!
What's hidden inside, so quirky and neat,
A sandwich of stories, both humble and sweet.

Savory Stories

Gather 'round, folks, for tales from the pan,
Hot and toasty, the best that they can.
With cheese made of dreams, melt in your heart,
And bacon of laughter, an artful tart.

Each layer's a journey, a flavor to chew,
Onions of antics, a laugh or two.
Ketchup of chaos drips down the sides,
Each savory story, where happiness hides.

So let's stack our sandwiches, one on the next,
With quirky fillings, we're truly perplexed.
A banquet of chuckles, a feast full of fun,
These savory stories, there's plenty for everyone.

The Savory Truth

Between the bread, a story lies,
With layers of laughs and sweet surprise.
Lettuce giggles, tomatoes cheer,
In this crazy mix, there's nothing to fear.

Creamy dreams spread far and wide,
A messy feast where flavors collide.
Pickles dance, mustard sings,
Take a bite, and joy it brings.

In every crumb, a secret kept,
The joy of munching, no need to fret.
Celebrate quirks, relish the zest,
In this tasty tale, we are so blessed.

So stack it high, build it proud,
Craving fun, let flavors crowd.
For in every sandwich, truth you'll find,
Happiness is crafted, one slice at a time.

Gathered Around the Edges

Gathered around with smiles so wide,
Sides of humor, what a fun ride.
Buns full of laughter, mayo's delight,
Chunky and savory, oh what a sight.

Friends are the fixings, spread out on board,
Sharing tall tales that can't be ignored.
Bread's getting toasted, hearts feeling light,
As we munch through our stories, oh what a night!

Crunchy old tales with a crispy twist,
Sinking our teeth in, not a chance we'll miss.
Between every layer, bonds securely blend,
This feast on a table, where laughter won't end.

So let's feast together, no need to compete,
With flavors that dance in a whimsical beat.
Gathered around, the edges filled tight,
In our sandwich of friendship, all feels just right.

The Comfort of Wholesome Choices

In a ain't-a-bore sort of way,
A tangle of flavors decides to parlay.
Crunchy carrots, chunky spreads,
Making sure all hungry needs are fed.

Cheesy jokes on each layer lend,
A sprinkle of joy, our taste buds mend.
Avocado hugs tomatoes tight,
Creating comfort that feels just right.

Slicing up troubles, we'll pickle our woes,
In this hearty blend, laughter just grows.
With every bite, new stories unite,
In wholesome choices, there's pure delight.

So spread it thick like butter on toast,
Laughing and munching is what we love most.
Comfort awaits in each tasty bite,
Together we savor this whimsical night.

From Crust to Core

In crispy crusts and soft, warm cores,
Lies a tale of flavor, ripe with roars.
Lettuce wraps giggles in every fold,
A sandwich of stories, daring and bold.

Tomato's blush brings sweetness to chat,
Riding on toasty bread, imagine that!
Each crunch a giggle, each squish a grin,
Let's dig right in, the fun's about to begin!

Relishing moments, no room for dread,
Each bite a journey on laughter's bread.
Saucy adventures and peppery spice,
In this stack of joy, everything's nice.

So let's raise our sandwiches, a toast to the feast,
Where friendship and food mingle at least.
From crust to core, let laughter soar,
In every tasty layer, we crave more and more.

The Filling of Existence

In the lunchbox of our days,
Giggles and snacks dance and play.
Pickles and mustard twist and slide,
Adventures await, let's take a ride.

Silly sounds and jelly spills,
Chocolate whispers give us thrills.
Crunchy munchies sound the cheer,
Life's a picnic, let's grab a beer!

Lettuce laughing, tomatoes grin,
Each flavor brings a silly win.
The more we sprinkle, the more we find,
Joy is the filling we crafted with mind.

So spread that butter, make it thick,
With every layer, add a trick.
Grab a bite, don't sit and wait,
For the fun inside—don't hesitate!

Layers of Tomorrow

Imagine a stack of dreams so bright,
Layered with laughter, a pure delight.
A slice of sunshine, a dash of glee,
Spreading smiles, just wait and see.

Grabbing a hunk of silly fun,
With mustard smiles for everyone.
Each layer tells a funny tale,
As we munch our way along the trail.

Tomorrow's feast, a laughter stew,
Topped with pickles that jiggle too.
In the sandwich of what we see,
Each layer adds to what we can be.

So toast to moments that make us snicker,
With every bite, let joy grow quicker.
In this banquet, so full of surprise,
The layers of laughter shall never disguise.

Hidden Treasures Between Bread

Oh, what wonders snugly hide,
Between our doughy arms, they bide.
A cookie crumb, a stray cheese shred,
Whispers of joy where we are led.

Beneath the crust, mischief awaits,
With fruity giggles and silly fates.
Open your heart, let madness spread,
There's magic waiting where crumbs have tread.

Delightful bits of quirky cheer,
In the corners, wait the good vibes here.
Chomp on the bits, don't you mind,
For every crunch, new treasures we find.

So take a bite with zest and flair,
For the hidden spoils beneath the layers.
Each taste a story, a moment that's bright,
In this grand feast, let joy take flight!

The Essence Beneath the Crust

Crusty edges, but oh so sweet,
What's tucked inside can't be beat.
A swirl of flavors, a pinch of fun,
Join the feast, we're all here as one.

Here comes the cucumber, oh so bold,
With tales of laughter, yet untold.
A splash of mayo, a sprinkle of zest,
In each bite, we find our best.

Lost in the layers, where flavors entwine,
Embrace the silliness, let it shine.
Crispy giggles and savory dreams,
In every sandwich, joy bursts at the seams.

So take a nibble, let worries suspend,
For it's the essence that helps us mend.
With every munch, let friendship bloom,
In the crunch, we find our room!

Layered Journeys

In a world of crust and loaf,
We find joy in every trope.
Pickles whisper, tomatoes dance,
And mustard gives us all a chance.

From soggy bread to crunchy cheer,
Each bite reveals, we hold so dear.
Jelly laughs with peanut spread,
A symphony in every shred.

Lettuce layers, crinkled thoughts,
Happiness is what we've sought.
With every munch and every crunch,
We savor more than just our lunch.

So stack it high, don't be shy,
Each silly combo makes us fly.
In this banquet, let's confound,
For every layer, joy is found.

Bite-Sized Reflections

Cheese with grapes, a wild delight,
Twirling flavors in the night.
Bread's soft hug, a warm embrace,
In gourmet chaos, we find grace.

Cucumber smiles with a crunch,
While olives dance in a joyful bunch.
Every nibble tells a tale,
Of laughter caught in every grail.

Jam surprise and butter bliss,
A ridiculous, savory kiss.
In each layer, a twist unfolds,
Life's great banquet, so behold!

As we savor, let's be bold,
For these moments never grow old.
With humor smeared across the bread,
We feast on joy, enough said!

The Richness of Being

With relish on top, what a sight,
Building bites that burst with light.
Tomato slices grin and cheer,
Telling stories far and near.

Avocados spread their wisdom wide,
Crispy onions, our fun ride.
Each mouthful sings of joy and spice,
In this feast, we think twice.

A sprinkle of nuts, a dash of flair,
Taste the world without a care.
Bites of laughter, moments shared,
In this meal, we're fully paired.

So stack it up, don't hold back,
With flavors bold, we stay on track.
For richness blooms both inside and out,
In every layer, twist, and shout!

Centered Flavors

In the middle, a world so grand,
Silly mashups at our command.
Peanut butter, jelly dreams,
Life's odd combos burst at the seams.

From spicy mustard to sweet glaze,
Each flavor plays in joyful ways.
Crunch and chew, oh what a mix,
Beneath the bread, there's golden tricks.

Relish your quirks, stack them tall,
The more the layers, the more the call.
In every bite, a moment bright,
Turning dull days into delight.

So gather round for a happy tune,
As we munch beneath the moon.
With flavors vibrant, life's a dance,
In this sandwich, take the chance!

Hidden Depths

Beneath the crust, a curious weave,
Pickles and dreams, oh, what a reprieve!
Lettuce whispers secrets so bold,
With every crunch, a tale unfolds.

Tomato tears, juicy and bright,
Ketchup's laughter, a flavorful sight.
Bread holds it all, snug and tight,
In this layered wonder, pure delight.

Mustard spins yarns of glory and glee,
Chips on the side dance merrily.
Each bite a giggle, a zesty cheer,
In the sandwich's hug, we conquer our fear.

So take a big bite and let's not pretend,
What's inside makes it truly transcend!
For every filling, a grin in disguise,
A culinary journey, oh what a surprise!

Nourishing the Spirit

With every spread, a laugh is sown,
A hoagie of joy, we can't eat alone!
Crispy bacon, like laughter, it cracks,
Fueling the spirit, no room for lacks.

Creamy things hide, a wise old sage,
Whispering truths on a toasted stage.
Cucumber winks from its leafy lair,
In this banquet of silliness, who wouldn't dare?

So layer your troubles, toss them around,
In the warmth of a feast, joy can be found.
A sprinkle of nuts, or sprigs of thyme,
In every bite, life's silly rhyme!

Bite into laughter, season with cheer,
Sandwich your worries; they'll disappear!
From pickles to pesto, all flavors unite,
A comedic platter, a delicious bite!

A Culinary Life

Slices of moments piled up high,
Mayonnaise dreams, they never run dry.
Each element's quirky, unique in its way,
A culinary soap opera, come join the fray!

Bread's the foundation, sturdy and proud,
It holds our mishaps, our hopes, and the crowd.
Between these layers, oh what a blend,
With savory stories that never quite end.

We feast on the laughter, we munch on the fun,
With every new flavor, there's plenty to shun.
Life's tasty morsels, a glorious mix,
A buffet of chaos, with humorous kicks!

So pack up your troubles in buns all around,
Let's relish the moments, let joy abound.
For every fresh layer, a reason to cheer,
In this sandwich of life, absurdities steer!

Bits of Joy in Every Bite

Bite into joy, flavors collide,
Crunching on giggles, all dreams inside.
A dash of what's silly, a sprinkle of fun,
Every munch brings laughter, second to none.

The cheese melts softly, like hearts that meet,
Together we savor, an amusing treat.
Jalapeños kickstart a riotous cheer,
In the banquet of life, we gather near.

Wrap up those quips in a tortilla snug,
Every bite's a hug, warm and snug.
On this platter of moments, we joyously unite,
Finding bits of delight, in every bite!

So stack it all high, hold nothing back,
In this culinary caper, let's stay on track.
For each squishy morsel, let laughter ignite,
In the whimsy of flavor, everything's right!

Flavorful Footprints

In a world of thick jam and thin bread,
We wander through crumbs of thoughts in our head.
Pickles and mustard, a blend that's bizarre,
Each step leaves a taste, like a food truck bazaar.

We juggle our choices, a lunchroom ballet,
Banana peels slip; it's a slippery play.
Lettuce on top, but it's mayo below,
Life's just as messy as nachos in tow.

With each bite we take, we laugh and we munch,
Gather 'round the table, let's share the good crunch.
Tomato sauce drips on a whimsical plate,
In this feast of existence, we all celebrate.

So throw on the toppings, let flavors collide,
With mustard and relish, there's no need to hide.
From cheese to the bread, we'll swirl and we'll spin,
Embracing the stuffing that bubbles within.

Beyond the Edges

Between toasty borders, where secrets reside,
We find joy and laughter, with friends by our side.
Crusty adventures, not always so neat,
Imperfectly shaped, but oh, so sweet.

With bites of uncertainty, we dance and we sway,
Each squishy moment, a comical display.
Avocado dreams and a sprinkle of fun,
Mix in some chaos, and watch how we run.

From chips on the side to the soup in the bowl,
Each taste tells a story, it nourishes the soul.
Let's savor the crannies, the dips, and the fuss,
In this culinary jest, we find joy in the rust.

So lift up your sandwich, let's share a good laugh,
With every odd flavor, we craft our own path.
Beyond each horizon, new combos await,
In the pantry of life, let's poke and create!

What Holds Us Together

With layers aplenty, we gather like glue,
Every odd pairing is vibrant and true.
Peanut butter hugs jelly with glee,
It's all a reflection of you and of me.

The cheese and the crackers, a match made in bliss,
Each flavor we add, like a savory kiss.
Together we're stronger, that's quite the delight,
As laughter and tang blend into the night.

So spread out the memories, slather on cheer,
In this smorgasbord, there's nothing to fear.
A dash of adventure, a scoop of the zest,
In the heart of our sandwich, we surely are blessed.

With crumbs on our shirts, we merrily chime,
Embracing each oddity, one bite at a time.
From the bread to the fillings, it's all a big show,
For what binds us most is the joy that we sow!

Origins of Comfort

In a kitchen of chaos, where laughter is stirred,
Salty and sweet blend with each spoken word.
The toast pops with stories, we're hungry for chat,
Each layer a memory, how about that?

A pinch of the past, a dollop of fate,
With kitchen disasters, we patiently wait.
A splash of old pickle juice makes us grin,
In flavors of comfort, good times begin.

From soggy sandwiches to gourmet cuisine,
We taste every moment, like what might have been.
Pick out the odd bits, let the smiles spread wide,
In every mishap, there's laughter inside.

So here's to the bites, both joyous and wild,
With each quirky sandwich, remember your child.
From mustard mishaps to jelly-run friends,
In the sandwich of living, the fun never ends.

The Harmony of Flavors

In the kitchen, chaos reigns,
Pickles dancing on the panes.
Tomato talks with a slice of cheese,
Together they jam with effortless ease.

Lettuce giggles, crunchy and bright,
While mustard squirts with all its might.
A symphony of tastes in a crusty shell,
Each bite a story, it's hard to tell.

Bite down deep, what do you find?
A pickle's joke that's one of a kind.
Bread may crumble, but spirits stay,
Laughter rises with each buffet.

So stack those layers, don't be shy,
With silly toppings that soar and fly.
In this dish, joy and taste collide,
In the sandwich world, we all abide.

The Art of Filling

Jelly swirls in a nutty sea,
A squish, a smear, pure jubilee.
Bread's a canvas, your dreams are art,
Slather it on, let flavors start.

A spoonful of zen, a dollop of cheer,
Adventures unfold with each smear.
Tomato chats, urging a spread,
While avocado dreams in green instead.

Sprinkle some leaves, herbs would be great,
With random bites that tempt fate.
The art of filling, a craft in play,
Mix and match in a scrumptious way.

So grab that loaf, and don't hesitate,
For laughter waits as you create.
With every crunch, the fun won't cease,
In the sandwich realm, we find our peace.

Morsels of Meaning

Crumbs scatter like secrets untold,
Bites rich in jest, flavors bold.
A scoop of joy, a smear of fun,
This sandwich life is never done.

Banana's break with a peanut twist,
In the lunchbox, they love to exist.
A mystery mix of sweet and spice,
Each nibble brings a bit of advice.

What's it all about? You might just ask,
The cream of the crop is the relevant task.
So gather your snacks, make a big scene,
With hearty laughs and a snack between.

In every layer, find a new scheme,
Between the bites, we build a dream.
Morsels of meaning, quirky yet grand,
In every crust lies a joyful hand.

Reflections on Taste and Time

Bread crumbles on the floor,
A picnic gone awry,
Mustard spills, a yellow sea,
Laughing at the sky.

Colors clash on paper plates,
The pickle has a grin,
Tomato winks, just a tease,
Let the munching begin!

Each bite a merry dance,
Cheese and ham will sway,
Add a dash of laughter,
As we munch the day away.

With each crunch a memory,
Crunchy tales are spun,
In the party of our palates,
Everyone can have some fun.

The Palette of Possibility.

In the fridge, a treasure chest,
Leftovers collide,
A peanut butter symphony,
With jelly by its side.

Carrot sticks parade around,
In a ranch-dipped affair,
While olives roll with laughter,
Not a worry, not a care.

Salty chips in a conga line,
Dance with salsa bright,
Tortilla shells shout 'olé!'
As flavors take to flight.

Creating art on crispy bread,
A masterpiece of fun,
Each ingredient a story,
In this sandwich we have won!

A Layered Existence

Two slices of thick delight,
Hiding joy within,
A stacked-up world of flavors,
Where chaos can begin.

Pickles jump and jive about,
As lettuce starts to sway,
The onion lends a sharp wit,
In this wacky buffet!

Tomato brings the drama,
While bread stays in the race,
Together they create a feast,
With giggles in each place.

A layered life runs deep,
With surprises on each bite,
Savor every crunch and munch,
In this culinary flight!

The Heart Between Two Slices

In the middle, there it lies,
A heart of creamy bliss,
Surrounded by the crusty walls,
Who knew it'd come to this?

Avocado dreams, so soft and green,
Nestled with a smile,
In this quirky sandwich world,
We'll savor it a while.

The punch of spicy mustard,
Elbows come to play,
While the radish grins and giggles,
As we munch the day away.

So raise your slice and toast it high,
To laughter, love, and fun,
For in this tasty venture,
We're always on the run!

The Palate of Purpose

In a world of flavors, we choose each bite,
Whipped cream dreams and mustard delight.
Pickles and jelly, a curious blend,
Each layer tells stories that twist and bend.

Onions bring tears, while cheese makes you grin,
A mystery wrapped, and the fun begins.
With peanut butter hugs and jellyfish jives,
It's the squishy middle where laughter thrives.

Bacon dances bold, and lettuce plays coy,
A culinary riddle, a feast of joy.
So flip that sandwich, see what you've got,
Gleeful surprises are simmering hot.

In this grand buffet, there's no need to fret,
Seize every morsel, don't hold back just yet.
For life's a smorgasbord, spread your cheer wide,
The colors of joy are the stuff we can't hide.

Between Two Worlds

Two slices embrace, then the chaos begins,
With ketchup in hand and mustard within.
Each topping a treasure, each crunch a delight,
In this flickering kitchen, what's wrong is just right.

Tuna fish tangles with chocolate delight,
King of the combos, an unusual sight.
Like socks on a rooster, it's silly yet grand,
In this strange banquet, we all take a stand.

Waffles meet burgers, a sweet-salty song,
Together they dance, they can't be wrong.
Pick your ingredients, let laughter unfold,
A savory tale waiting to be told.

So let's stack our dreams, layer them high,
With giggles and joy, we'll reach for the sky.
In the realm of the silly, where breadcrumbs fall,
We find our true selves, and we laugh through it all.

Heartfelt Compositions

From rye to baguette, each choice is a hug,
Tomato and mayo, wrapped snug as a bug.
A dash of chutzpah, a sprinkle of glee,
In this sandwich of wonders, we are truly free.

A sugar rush sunrise with ham on the side,
Each forkful is magic, come take a ride.
With whipped cream clouds and doughnut sunbeams,
We savor the moments, we live our dreams.

A salsa sensation that tickles the tongue,
With giggles and guacamole, we've only begun.
Let's layer our stories, let our fables expand,
In the joy of assembling, together we stand.

For every great sandwich holds secrets and fun,
With every odd mix, we all see the sun.
So raise up your forks and let laughter resound,
In this feast of existence, joy's always around.

Unraveled Delicacies

In kitchens we tumble, like flour in flight,
A swirl of odd flavors, oh what a sight!
Bologna and jelly, a riddle to chew,
In the carnival of snacks, we're all just passing through.

Sweet mustard whispers and sauerkraut jokes,
Amidst crumpled recipes and giggling folks.
Each bite brings a chuckle, a playful surprise,
In this world of mishaps, watch laughter arise.

A crab in a cupcake? What fun will it bring?
With giggles and crunching, we'll dance and we'll sing.
Let's munch on the madness, let whimsy take flight,
For each layer we're peeling uncovers delight.

So gather your toppings, unleash your wild side,
With whimsy on plates, there's nowhere to hide.
In this banquet of chaos, we revel and share,
For in our odd journeys, there's joy everywhere.

www.ingramcontent.com/pod-product-compliance
Lightning Source LLC
Chambersburg PA
CBHW072149200426
43209CB00051B/913